THE

UNDEFILED

ONE

The Ancient of Days

Who Trampled Decay

SAHAR SOLTANI

Copyright © 2025 Sahar Soltani

All rights reserved. No part of this book may be reproduced or transmitted in any form or by any means, electronic, mechanical, photocopying, recording, or otherwise, without prior written permission from the author, except in the case of brief quotations used in articles, reviews, or academic references.

This book is a work of spiritual nonfiction. All statements, ideas, interpretations, and theological reflections represent the author's personal study and spiritual understanding. Readers are encouraged to seek the Scriptures and the Spirit for personal discernment and revelation.

While legal authorship remains with the author, the truth and revelation within this book are not of human origin but rooted in the Word of YHWH. This scroll was written not from ambition, but from a sincere desire to align with the Scriptures and the Spirit, with reverence and care to avoid the false and limited interpretations that so often distort what was originally written.

All Scripture quotations in this work are rendered in restored form, referencing the original Hebrew, Aramaic and Greek texts as closely as possible. Every effort has been made to preserve Divine Names and original meanings including the restoration of **YHWH, Yeshua,** and other key terms where they were altered or obscured in mainstream translations. All usage falls under fair use guidelines and is offered respectfully for teaching and commentary.

Published by The Quiet Seer Press
Designed by Sahar Soltani
For inquiries: quietseerpress@outlook.com
ISBN: 978-1-0698031-0-8

To those who seek truth

and nothing but the whole truth

and who search for it

as for silver.

—S.S.

For if you call for intelligence,

lift up your voice for understanding,

If you seek her as silver,

and search for her as hidden treasures,

Then you understand fear of YHWH,

and find knowledge of Elohim.

—Proverbs 2:3-5

Author's Note

This scroll was not written to please men.
It was not fashioned in the halls of academia,
nor edited by the traditions of councils.

It was breathed out in the secret place,
before the Audience of One.

The only authority I cite is the Word of God.
When I speak of "Scripture,"
I speak of that which was breathed by the Spirit:
the Holy Writings preserved through the ages.

This includes the 66 books recognized today,
and also the ancient record known
as the Book of 1 Enoch:
the testimony of a man who walked with God
until he was no more. (Genesis 5:24)

Though traditions of men chose
to exclude his words,
heaven did not.
The Spirit affirmed Enoch's testimony
through the apostle Jude (Jude 1:14–15),
and the Spirit still bears witness today.

I do not seek validation from man.
I do not fear the traditions of men.
I fear only the Living Elohim, YHWH.

Every declaration in this scroll
stands upon the Scriptures alone,
and upon the breath of the Spirit who wrote them.

This scroll is written
not only for those who already believe,
but also for those who are seeking,
questioning,
wrestling,
and longing for the truth
they were never shown.

It is written for the wounded.
The misled.
The lost.
The ones who were told lies about the Holy One.

It is written for you, whoever you are,
that you may see the Undefiled One rightly,
and glorify Him as He deserves.
For He deserves all the glory, honor,
and majesty.

Prologue: The Search for Holiness

From the earliest days of my faith,
I was taught that Yeshua came into the world
as a man,
that He was fully human, just like us.
I accepted this without question,
because it was what I had always heard
and what was also written.
Yet deep inside, something unsettled me.

How could the Holy One of Israel, YHWH Himself,
enter into human flesh
and experience the filth of fallen mortality?
Could the Pure One truly participate in the decay
and corruption that marks the post-Eden world?

It did not make sense to me.
Not because I doubted His humility.
Not because I doubted His humanity.
But because I could not accept that the undefiled God
would willingly subject Himself to defilement that
had nothing to do with redemption.

Pain, thirst, hunger,
these sufferings I understood.

They were necessary for Him to fulfill His mission,
to bear the weight of sin,
to redeem us from death.

But meaningless bodily corruption,
processes that symbolized the curse of death,
had no place in the life of the Lamb who would be
"without blemish and without spot."

I realized that to honor Yeshua rightly,
I could no longer accept shallow assumptions.

This book is the result of that sacred wrestling.
It began not in study, but in quiet revelation,
when YHWH opened my mind to a mystery:
that Yeshua, even in flesh,
remained utterly and completely undefiled.
From there, the journey unfolded,
through Scripture,
through pattern recognition,
and piece by piece,
the Word confirmed what He had first revealed.

This is not merely a theological study.
It is an act of worship.
An offering to the One who is **Holy, Holy, Holy,**
even in the likeness of man.

Introduction: Why This Matters

When we speak of Yeshua's manifestation in flesh,
we often repeat the phrase:
"fully God and fully man."

Yet too often,
we recite these words without pausing to consider
their true weight.

If He is YHWH in flesh,
the embodiment of absolute holiness,
then every aspect of His earthly experience
must align perfectly with His divine nature.

Yeshua did not come to earth to lose His holiness.
He came to fulfill all righteousness.

Everything He chose to experience:
from hunger to thirst,
from pain to death itself,
had a direct purpose in the redemption of mankind.

Nothing He endured was random.
Nothing He submitted to was meaningless.
Nothing He allowed could violate His nature

as the Holy One.

This book argues that Yeshua,
while truly taking on flesh,
did not participate in the fallen corruption of mortality
beyond what was necessary for our salvation.

In particular, we will explore how His life was free
not only from moral sin,
but also from the physical markers of decay,
including the bodily waste that testifies
to fallen corruption,
and that unbelievers—Muslims and others—have
used to slander the holiness of my God.

This matters profoundly.

Because to misunderstand His purity
is to misunderstand His sacrifice.
And to misunderstand His sacrifice
is to diminish the glory of His love.

This book will walk through Scripture,
through Scriptural reflection,
and reasoned reflection on the nature of Eden,
mortality, and the resurrection.

And through the revelation of the Spirit
to recover a vision of Yeshua
as the perfectly Undefiled One.

My prayer is that as you journey
through these pages,
you too will see Him more clearly,
and worship Him more purely,
the Holy Lamb who remained flawless,
even while wearing flesh.

If we are to worship Him rightly,
we must behold Him rightly.
Not through the assumptions of man,
but through the revelation of the Ruach haQodesh.

Let us now turn our hearts and our eyes
to the mystery of the Word becoming flesh:
to the Undefiled One,
who wore flesh without corruption.

Table of Contents

Author's Note………………………………..……..vii
Prologue: The Search for Holiness………………......ix
Introduction: Why This Matters……………………..xi

Chapter 1: The Undefiled Body…………………….1
Chapter 2: The Lost Realm of the Undefiled…………7
Chapter 3: The Purpose of the Body………………...15
Chapter 4: The Death That Could Not Hold Him…….
………………………………………………....19
Chapter 5: The Undefiled Resurrection……………..25
Chapter 6: The Remnant of the Incorruptible…………31
Chapter 7: The Final Unveiling of Incorruption………
……………………………………………..37
Testimony of the Word: The Undefiled One……….43
Glory Wore Flesh: A Final Reflection on the
Undefiled One……………………………….............47
Testimony from the Hidden Scrolls…………………57
Final Seal……………………………………………..59
Acknowledgment…………………………...............63
About the Author………………………………….....65

Chapter 1: The Undefiled Body

We were made in His image,
but we were never Him.

We carry a likeness,
but not the fullness of His eternal nature.

When Yeshua came into the world,
He did not come to become human by essence,
but to clothe Himself in human form.

"In the beginning was the Word,"
"and the Word was with God,"
"and the Word was God." (John 1:1)

And the Word became flesh,
and dwelt among us. (John 1:14)

But the Word never ceased to be God,
not for a moment,
not for a breath,
not even in the womb.

A body was prepared for Him:
"Sacrifice and offering You did not desire,

but a body You have prepared for Me."
(Hebrews 10:5)

A body untouched by Adam's curse,
woven by the Holy Spirit in the virgin's womb.
(Luke 1:35)
Holy from conception.
Holy to the end.

He walked among the corrupted,
but remained undefiled.
He touched the broken,
but was never contaminated.

He shared in flesh and blood:
"Since the children have flesh and blood,
He too shared in their humanity…" (Hebrews 2:14)

but without ever taking on the corruption
that ruled fallen flesh.

He tasted hunger,
thirst,
fatigue,
pain,
but not corruption.

"He was tempted in every way, just as we are, yet without sin." (Hebrews 4:15)

He bore weakness for our sake,
but not decay for His own.

Decay belongs to sin.
Corruption is the offspring of rebellion. (Romans 5:12)

But the Second Adam,
the True Son,
the I AM in flesh,
carried no sin in His blood.
Carried no corruption in His bones.

"You will not allow Your Holy One
to see decay." (Acts 2:27)

He chose to feel the limits of flesh,
but the grave could not limit Him.
He entered death,
but death could not hold Him.

Because death only owns what it corrupts.
And He was incorruptible.

He became flesh,
but flesh never became Him.

He clothed Himself in a body,
but His Spirit remained sovereign.

"He made Himself nothing,
taking the very nature of a servant,
being made in human likeness." (Philippians 2:7)

Likeness.
Not fallen substance.
Not corrupted being.

He was,
and is,
and is to come
the Undefiled One.
The Holy One.
The Untouchable Flame
wrapped in the appearance of man.

Even Enoch, the seventh from Adam,
foresaw the coming of the Holy One in judgment:
"Behold, the Lord comes with ten thousands of His
saints, to execute judgment upon all…"
(Jude 1:14, echoed from 1 Enoch 1:9)

Enoch saw Him
not as a fallen man,
but as the Righteous Judge robed in glory.

The body of Messiah was not a prison.
It was a vessel,
prepared for the altar.

He laid it down willingly. (John 10:18)
And He took it up again,
glorified,
imperishable. (Luke 24:39)

He is the First and the Last.
The Visible Image of the Invisible God.
(Colossians 1:15)

He walked among us in human form,
but never ceased to be the I AM.

Chapter 2: The Lost Realm of the Undefiled

Before corruption entered the world,
there was Eden.

Not merely a garden.
Not merely a paradise of nature.

Eden was a realm:
a supernatural overlap of heaven and earth,
where the breath of YHWH infused every leaf,
every river,
every living thing.

It was the place where the visible and the invisible
walked hand in hand.
Where dust wore glory.
Where man stood undefiled
not by strength,
but by communion.

The first Adam was not created for death.
He was formed for life:
life untainted by decay,
life untouched by corruption.

He bore the image of Elohim
not as a fragile reflection,
but as a living vessel of His presence.

"God saw all that He had made,
and it was very good." (Genesis 1:31)

Very good.
Not corrupted.
Not mortal as we know it now.

The dust of the ground was crowned
with the breath of life. (Genesis 2:7)
The man was clothed,
not in perishable garments,
but in the radiance of fellowship
with the Ancient of Days.

Eden was undefiled,
and so was the body of man.

No rot.
No aging.
No sickness.
No death.

Creation was still singing the original song,

pure,
whole,
alive.

But a serpent spoke
and the song faltered.

When Adam fell,
defilement entered.

Corruption sank into the bones of man.
Decay infected the dust.
Death became the law written in every cell.

"By one man sin entered into the world,
and death by sin;
and so death passed upon all men, for that all have
sinned." (Romans 5:12)

The glory that once clothed Adam faded.
The body that once shone with life began to wither.
The earth itself groaned under the weight of betrayal.
(Romans 8:20–22)

Dust to dust,
ashes to ashes
became the fate of all

who bore the mark of the fallen Adam.

The gateway to Eden closed.
The cherubim stood watch with flaming sword.
(Genesis 3:24)
Not in cruelty,
but in mercy,
to prevent immortal corruption from sealing
mankind's doom forever.

Eden was lost.
The realm of the undefiled was sealed.
The image of God in man was marred.

Not destroyed
but defiled.

And every child of Adam since that day
was born under the sentence of death,
born with the seed of corruption already sown deep
in flesh and bone.

No matter how righteous a man tried to be,
his body still marched toward the grave.
No matter how holy the heart,
the dust still demanded its return.

Thus the promise was whispered:
A Seed would come.
A new Adam.
An Undefiled One.

"I will put enmity between you and the woman,
and between your seed and her Seed;
He shall bruise your head,
and you shall bruise His heel." (Genesis 3:15)

One
not born of Adam's corrupted line.
One
not stained by rebellion.
One
not sentenced to death by inheritance.

The Undefiled One would come
not just to save souls,
but to redeem bodies.
Not just to forgive sins,
but to reverse corruption.
Not just to offer escape,
but to reopen Eden.

He would wear flesh
without defilement.

He would die
without decay.
He would rise
without corruption.

And in Him,
the lost glory of Eden would live again,
not in myth,
but in blood,
in bone,
in Spirit.

Yeshua is not merely the Restorer of fellowship.
He is the Restorer of the Undefiled.

The New Creation does not float above the earth.
It invades it.
It heals it.
It remakes it.

The New Jerusalem does not call us to escape.
It calls Eden to descend.

"Behold, the tabernacle of God is with men,
and He will dwell with them,
and they shall be His people,
and God Himself will be with them

and be their God." (Revelation 21:3)

If we do not understand Eden,
we cannot understand why Yeshua
had to be undefiled.
We cannot understand why His body
had to be pure,
His blood incorruptible,
His resurrection bodily and eternal.

He is the Undefiled One,
restoring the lost realm,
remaking the fallen body,
reopening the gates of Eden.

Let us now turn our eyes back
to the Holy Vessel prepared
before the foundation of the world:
the Undefiled Body,
given for the redemption of dust
and soul alike.

Chapter 3: The Purpose of the Body

He did not come merely to walk among us.
He came to redeem us.
To tear the veil that separated flesh from Spirit.

A sacrifice was required.
But not just any sacrifice.
Not the blood of bulls or goats. (Hebrews 10:4)

The law demanded blood.
Justice demanded life for life.

But heaven demanded something greater:
an offering without blemish.
(Exodus 12:5; 1 Peter 1:19)

An undefiled Lamb.
A body prepared from before the foundations of the world. (Revelation 13:8)

Not stained by Adam's rebellion.
Not corrupted by man's sin.

A pure vessel,
carrying the very life of YHWH Himself.

"The life is in the blood,"
the Scripture declares. (Leviticus 17:11)

And His blood was holy.
Pulsing with the incorruptible Spirit.
Unmixed with the corruption of fallen man.

He could not offer what was already dead.
He offered what was ever-living.

He did not come to reform humanity.
He came to create a New Humanity:
a rebirth through His own death.

"For as in Adam all die,
so in Messiah all will be made alive."
(1 Corinthians 15:22)

The body was the instrument.
The blood was the river.
The Spirit was the fire.

He laid down His undefiled body willingly.
(John 10:18)
No man took it from Him.

And because He was without sin,
death could not hold Him.

"It was impossible for death to keep its hold on Him." (Acts 2:24)

He bore our sins upon His body. (1 Peter 2:24)
Yet His Spirit remained without spot.
Without wrinkle.
Without decay.

He became the bridge
between earth and heaven,
between dust and divinity.

His body was not conquered.
It was the door.

"I am the Door," He said. (John 10:9)

And through the torn veil of His flesh,
we now have access to the Holy of Holies.
(Hebrews 10:20)

The Word became flesh
so that flesh could return to the Word.

Chapter 4: The Death That Could Not Hold Him

He did not taste death because of weakness.
He tasted death because of willing surrender.

No man took His life from Him.
He laid it down by His own authority. (John 10:18)

The grave opened its mouth,
expecting to devour Him
as it had devoured all sons of Adam.

But death did not know
that this One was not born of Adam's corruption.
This One carried no sin in His veins.
No decay in His bones.
No rebellion in His spirit.

"It was impossible for death to keep its hold on Him."
(Acts 2:24)

The grave could not hold what it could not corrupt.
Death could not own what had no debt.

He bore our sins in His body upon the tree.

(1 Peter 2:24)
But the sins were not His own.
They clung to Him for judgment,
but they could not penetrate Him for defilement.

*"You will not abandon my soul to Sheol,
nor will You allow Your Holy One to see corruption."*
(Psalm 16:10, Acts 2:27)

Corruption is the curse of sin.
Decay is the evidence of death's dominion.

But He was, is, and is to come the Living One.
Blameless in life.
Blameless in death.
Blameless forevermore.

Even in the silence of the tomb,
His flesh did not rot.
His frame did not fall apart.
The Holy One remained holy.
The Living Word remained incorruptible.
The Undefiled One remained undefiled.

Three days and three nights,
the world waited in darkness.

But the Holy One slept in the Spirit,
not in decay.

And on the third day,
life surged back into the vessel
that death could not defile.

"I am the Resurrection and the Life." (John 11:25)

Not only did He rise —
He rose incorruptible.

He rose as the Firstborn from the dead.
(Colossians 1:18)
The Seed of the New Creation.
The proof that death had been swallowed up
in victory. (1 Corinthians 15:54)

He is the Lamb who was slain,
yet stands alive.
The Pierced One,
yet the Undefeated.

He died by choice.
He rose by His own authority,
by the divine plan preconceived
before the foundation of creation.

Not as a prisoner released,
but as the Author of Life
reclaiming His vessel.

For He is the Resurrection
and the Life.
And death could not imprison
what was already eternal.
And because He rules over death itself,
those who are born of Him
shall also live.

Death was a tool in His hand,
not a prison around His soul.

And because He lives,
those who are born of Him
shall also live.

Righteous.
Undefiled.
Free.

The grave was forced to release
what it could not hold.
The body that death could not corrupt
emerged in power,

glorified,
eternal.

Now we turn to gaze upon the mystery
of His resurrection,
and the glory of the Undefiled Body
that death could not decay
and time could not diminish.

Chapter 5: The Undefiled Resurrection

The stone was rolled away,
but not to let Him out.
It was to reveal to the world
that death had lost its prey.

He rose
not as a ghost,
not as a memory,
but in the fullness of a glorified body.

"Touch Me and see," He said,
"for a spirit does not have flesh and bones
as you see I have." (Luke 24:39)

This was no illusion.
No mere spiritual appearance.
The Firstborn from the dead stood before them:
the same body that was pierced,
now glorified beyond corruption.

The wounds remained,
not as marks of defeat,
but as banners of victory.

The resurrected body of Yeshua was physical
yet transformed.
Solid
yet transcendent.
Recognizable
yet radiant with a life that death
could never touch again.

"He breathed on them and said,
'Receive the Holy Spirit.'" (John 20:22)

The Breath of the New Creation began to blow
from the lungs of the Risen One.

His resurrection was not merely a reversal of death,
it was the unveiling of incorruptibility.

The grave was not just defeated.
It was emptied of its claim against the undefiled.

"Christ has indeed been raised from the dead,
the firstfruits of those who have fallen asleep."
(1 Corinthians 15:20)

Firstfruits.
The beginning of a new harvest.
The sign that a new creation had already begun.

Just as His body rose imperishable,
so too shall the bodies of those born of Him.
"Sown in corruption, raised in incorruption;
sown in dishonor, raised in glory;
sown in weakness, raised in power."
(1 Corinthians 15:42–43)

He rose not only for Himself.
He rose as the guarantee
that those united to Him
shall also put on immortality.

This is the hope of the remnant,
not escape into a spirit realm,
but full redemption of the body.
A resurrection into incorruption.
A return to the original design:
man walking with Yahweh,
undefiled by decay.

For Yeshua is not just the Savior of souls.
He is the Redeemer of bodies.
The Restorer of the fallen creation.

"For we eagerly await a Savior from heaven,
the Lord Yeshua Messiah,

who will transform our lowly bodies
to be like His glorious body." (Philippians 3:20–21)

He is the Pattern.
He is the Firstborn.
He is the Proof.

The Undefiled One rose in an undefiled body.
And by His resurrection,
He has broken the curse for all who are in Him.

This is not myth.
Not symbol.
Not metaphor.

It is the cornerstone of our faith.

"If Messiah has not been raised, your faith is futile;
you are still in your sins." (1 Corinthians 15:17)

But He has been raised.
And He reigns.
The Living Word,
clothed in glory,
undiminished by death.

Behold Him, the Undefiled Resurrection.

The New Beginning.
The Firstborn of many brothers and sisters.
The Victor over Sheol.
The Seed of the incorruptible kingdom.

And those who are born of Him
shall be like Him.

Yet even now,
while we await the redemption of our mortal frames,
we are called to live as those
who belong to the incorruptible.

We are called to wear the mark
of the New Creation,
even while still walking among the dying.

Let us now turn to the call of the remnant,
the children of the Undefiled One.

Chapter 6: The Remnant of the Incorruptible

They are not many.
They are not loud.
They are not crowned by the world.

But they are marked,
marked by the Breath of the Risen One,
sealed by the life of the Undefiled.

They walk through a dying world,
but their steps are ordered
by the King of the Universe,
Melech haOlam.

They carry within them the scent of a Kingdom
not built by human hands.
Their loyalty is not to dust and decay,
but to the Everlasting One,
the Ancient of Days.

The remnant is those who have seen Him,
not with the eyes of flesh,
but with the eyes of the spirit.
They have beheld the Undefiled One,

the Firstborn from the dead,
and they cannot return to the corruption
of what is passing away.

"My sheep hear My voice,
and I know them,
and they follow Me." (John 10:27)

The remnant follows the voice of the Living Word.
The voice of El Roi:
the God who sees them
even when the world overlooks them.

They hunger not for the bread of this world,
but for the incorruptible manna that descends
from the heart of YHWH Tsavaot,
the Lord of Hosts.

They carry death in their mortal bodies,
yet life in their veins.
"Though outwardly we are wasting away,
yet inwardly, we are being renewed day by day."
(2 Corinthians 4:16)

The remnant is not preserved by strength of flesh,
but by the power of the Undefiled One
who breathed incorruptible life into dust.

They await not the accolades of men,
but the appearing of the Pierced One,
whose voice will split the heavens
and call the dead to rise.

"For the trumpet will sound,
and the dead will be raised incorruptible,
and we shall be changed." (1 Corinthians 15:52)

They groan inwardly,
waiting for the adoption,
the redemption of their bodies.

"We eagerly await a Savior,
the Lord Yeshua Messiah,
who will transform our lowly bodies
to be like His glorious body." (Philippians 3:20–21)

They are strangers here.
Ambassadors of an incorruptible Kingdom.
Living letters,
written not with ink,
but with the Spirit of the Living God.

They do not belong to Babylon.
They do not feast at the table of corruption.

They do not bow to the gods of decay.

Their allegiance is to the Lamb who was slain.
Their hope is in the Risen King.
Their longing is for the restoration of all things.

They walk by a different rhythm.
They breathe a different air.
They shine with a different light.

For the same Spirit who raised Yeshua
from the dead
dwells in them now.

"If the Spirit of Him who raised Yeshua
from the dead dwells in you,
He who raised Messiah will also give life
to your mortal bodies through His Spirit
who dwells in you." (Romans 8:11)

They live between two worlds:
tasting the incorruptible Kingdom now,
while groaning for the full unveiling to come.

They are the sons and daughters of resurrection.
The heirs of the New Creation.
The remnant of the incorruptible.

They are not perfect.
But they are purified.
Not flawless in flesh.
But faultless by the Blood.

They do not walk by sight.
They walk by the promise of the Unfailing One,
the Melech haOlam,
the Everlasting King.

And they will not be forgotten.

El Roi sees them.
The Ancient of Days remembers their tears.
YHWH Tsavaot commands His angels
concerning them.

And soon,
the sky will split,
and the cry of the Risen One will shake the dust,
and the remnant shall rise
clothed in the incorruptible,
crowned by the Undefiled One Himself.

They are the remnant,
sealed by the Breath of the Risen One,

marked by the life of the Undefiled.

Yet even as they walk among the dying,
their eyes are lifted beyond the veil.

They await not merely survival,
but the complete unveiling of incorruption.

For the promise is not only inward renewal.
The promise is full restoration:
body, soul, and spirit,
woven together again in glory.

The Ancient of Days has spoken it.
Melech haOlam has decreed it.
YHWH Tsavaot will bring it to pass.

And when the trumpet sounds,
the dust of the faithful shall rise
clothed not in mortal garments,
but in the garments of immortality.

Let us now turn our hearts
to the final unveiling—
the redemption of all things.

Chapter 7: The Final Unveiling of Incorruption

It descends
not as an escape from earth,
but as the healing of earth.
The restoration of what was lost.

"And I saw the holy city, New Jerusalem,
coming down out of heaven from God,
prepared as a bride adorned for her husband."
(Revelation 21:2)

This is Eden reborn.
This is Eden restored.

Not merely paradise regained
but paradise transfigured.
The overlap of heaven and earth once severed,
now united forever.

The gateway that was closed by the flaming sword
of the cherubim (Genesis 3:24)
is thrown open by the blood of the Undefiled One.

No longer exile.

No longer separation.
No longer death.

The New Jerusalem is not an escape from creation.
It is the marriage of the divine and the earthly,
the healing of all that was broken.

The Tree of Life, once guarded and forbidden,
now blooms at the center of the City.
Its leaves heal the nations.
Its fruit sustains the remnant.
Its roots drink from the river of life.

"On either side of the river stood the tree of life,
bearing twelve crops of fruit,
yielding its fruit every month.
And the leaves of the tree are for the healing
of the nations." (Revelation 22:2)

The City shines not by the light of sun or moon,
but by the unveiled glory of the Ancient of Days.
The Lamb is its lamp.
The Breath of El Elyon fills every street with life.

"The city has no need of the sun or the moon
to shine on it,
for the glory of God gives it light,

and its lamp is the Lamb." (Revelation 21:23)

There is no decay here.
No rot.
No mourning behind locked doors.

The meek inherit the renewed earth.
The pure in heart see YHWH face to face.

"For here we have no lasting city,
but we seek the city that is to come."
(Hebrews 13:14)

The City is not just a destination.
It is a Person.
It is a Presence.

It is the dwelling of the Undefiled One
among the redeemed.
It is Eden resurrected,
baptized in everlasting fire,
clothed in incorruptibility.

The remnant is called up by the Master.
They walk upon the ground
that has been made new.
They drink from rivers that cannot be polluted.

They breathe air untainted by sin.

They are home.
Home as it was meant to be.
Home as Eden once sang.
Home as the Undefiled One has decreed.

"Behold, I make all things new." (Revelation 21:5)

The former things are passed away.
The curse is broken.
The defilement is undone.

The nations bring their honor into the City.
The kings lay down their crowns before the Lamb.
Every wound is healed.
Every tear wiped away
by the hand of Melech haOlam,
the King of the Universe.

This is not mythology.
This is not allegory.

This is the ultimate unveiling of the promise
first whispered in Eden,
fulfilled by the blood of the Undefiled One.
Sealed by the Spirit of the Living God.

The City is not crowned by its walls.
It is crowned by its King.

At the center stands the Throne,
the Seat of the Undefiled One.
The source of life.
The river of restoration.
The government of everlasting righteousness.

Let us lift our eyes higher still
toward the Great White Throne
of the glorious Undefiled King.

"They will see His face,
and His Name will be on their foreheads.
There will be no more night.
They will not need the light of a lamp
or the light of the sun,
*for **YHWH Elohim** will give them light.*
And they will reign forever and ever."
(Revelation 22:4–5)

Testimony of the Word: The Undefiled One

He who knew no sin
was made to be sin for us
yet He remained without sin.

"For such a Kohĕn Gadol (High Priest)
was fitting for us,
set-apart, innocent, undefiled,
separated from sinners and
exalted above the shamayim (heavens)."
—Iḇrim (Hebrews) 7:26

"Who committed no sin
nor was deceit found in His mouth."
—1 Kĕpha (Peter) 2:22

"In Him there is no sin."
—1 Yoḥanan (John) 3:5

"A Lamb without blemish and without spot."
—1 Kĕpha (Peter) 1:19

"The prince of the world is coming,
but he has nothing in Me."
—Yoḥanan (John) 14:30

"You do not leave My being in She'ol (realm of the dead) nor allow Your Kind One to see corruption."
—Tehillim (Psalm) 16:10 / Ma'aseh (Acts) 2:27

He was tried in every way, like us
yet without sin.
—Iḇrim (Hebrews) 4:15

"You made His grave with the wrong,
and with the rich at His death,
because He had done no violence,
nor was deceit in His mouth."
—Yesha'yahu (Isaiah) 53:9

"For He made Him who knew no sin
to be sin for us,
so that in Him we might become
the righteousness of Elohim."
—Qorintiyim Bĕt (2 Corinthians) 5:21

"And the Word became flesh and dwelt among us,
and we saw His esteem,
esteem as of an only brought-forth of a father,
complete in favor and truth."
—Yoḥanan (John) 1:14

He is the Word made flesh
and the Word cannot be corrupted.

He took on the likeness of men
but never the defilement of fallen man.

His flesh experienced death
but not decay.
His body was laid in the tomb
but never broken by corruption.
He rose again
not as dust returning to dust
but as the Incorruptible One
full of esteem and everlasting purity.

Glory Wore Flesh: A Final Reflection on the Undefiled One

Chesed—
the only Love fully defined,
fulfilled,
and completed
by YHWH alone.

And that body,
born out of chesed,
was not born of sin.
Was not shaped by corruption.
Was not bound by the limitations
of fallen flesh.

If Yeshua could become fully man
without inheriting sin,
then He could also take on a body
without inheriting decay.

He could bleed,
but never decay.
He could speak,
but never lie.

He could hunger,
but never crave fulfillment.
He could thirst,
but never for righteousness.

And yes,
even if He could defecate,
He may have chosen not to.

Not because the act itself is sin,
but because He bore no waste.
He solely bore glory.
YHWH Qadosh is He.

So do not defile the Qadosh One
by insisting
through faulty human lens
that He bore what He came to abolish.

For true Glory does not rot.
It does not excrete.
It sanctifies.
It consumes.
YHWH Esh Okhlah—
the Consuming Fire.

This wasn't a man struggling

to maintain purity.
This was Purity wearing skin,
for the sake of ungrateful mankind.

He didn't come to prove
that He could be like us.
He came to expose the lie
we've been living—
life outside Eden,
enslaved by sin,
eroded by decay,
drenched in shame.

He came to reveal that we
were always meant to be:
Unbroken,
Unveiled,
Unashamed,
Overcomers.

Not ruled by darkness,
but crowned with authority.
Not beneath pre-defeated, fallen powers,
but made to reign over them.

He came,
not as a created elohim

mimicking the Uncreated Elohim,
but as YHWH Elohei Qedem,
the God of Eternity,
redefining humanity
by embodying His own Divinity.

Selah.

Even the one chosen to mother Him,
Mary,
knew He wasn't from her.

"But Mary treasured up all these things, pondering them in her heart."
—Luke 2:19
"But His mother treasured all these things in her heart."
—Luke 2:51

Let's be clear:
Yeshua did not need a mother.
He created Mary.

But for the sake of fulfilling prophecy,
and entering time,
the very God of Mary
chose to be carried

by the very womb
He Himself had formed.

She wasn't the source of His divinity.
She was the vessel for His humanity.

Even she knew,
she wasn't raising a prophet.
She was beholding her Creator,
in the form of a child.

Mary knew He was not like "us."
Not just because an angel said so,
but because everything about Him
defied the ordinary.

She didn't try to explain Him.
She didn't speak it out loud.
Because what she saw
couldn't be reduced
to created words:
language born of earth,
formed for the finite,
too small to hold the Infinite.

She wasn't just pregnant.
She was perplexed by purity.

This wasn't just a gifted child.
She knew.
She carried the Uncreated One in flesh.
And her spirit whispered what her lips
couldn't yet say:
"This Child is not from here."

And even now,
the womb that once held Him:
worships Him.

Because she knew:
He did not come from her.
He came from before her.

Perhaps morning sickness was absent.
Perhaps there was no natural explanation
for what she felt growing within her,
because from the very beginning,
it wasn't natural procreation,
but Divine bestowment.

She was overshadowed by the Spirit,
and she knew:
She wasn't carrying a man
becoming holy.
She was carrying

Holiness itself.

That's why she said,

"My soul magnifies the Lord...
for the Mighty One has done great things for me.
Holy is His name."
—Luke 1:46–49

She didn't need proof.
She carried the Presence.

He didn't borrow our brokenness.
He didn't inherit Adam's stain.
He didn't assume our flaws as a necessity.
He wore flesh
but not the fall.

Because Glory wasn't conceived by man's seed.
Glory wasn't born into
Adam's chain of inheritance.
He was the Qadosh Seed—
not the product of it.
—Galatians 3:16

So the law of decay couldn't govern Him.
The curse of sin couldn't mark Him.

And the dirt of death had no claim on His frame.

Yes, He bled.
But His blood was undefiled.

Yes, He suffered.
But His suffering was chosen,
not forced,
not birthed.

Yes, He walked among iniquity,
surrounded by corruption,
immersed in the stain of a fallen world.

But He was never tainted.
Never defiled.
Never corrupted.

For He was Righteousness Himself:
YHWH Tsidkenu.

And now,
this is not the mystery they defend
when reason collapses
and contradictions thrive.

This is what you call

holy distinction,
where reverence births understanding,
and Truth doesn't contradict itself.

Therefore, His Name,
the only Name
given under Heaven,
to Earth,
beneath the Earth,
to time,
and within the limitations
of all created hosts,

is the Name
carrying a Name
only He knows.
—Revelation 19:12

Testimony from the Hidden Scrolls

(1 Enoch and 4 Ezra)

"And the Chosen One shall in those days
sit on My throne,
and from the mouth of His truth
He shall cause sinners to pass away.
He shall never deny the Name of YHWH of Hosts.
Before the sun and the signs were created,
His Name was spoken before YHWH of Hosts."
—1 Enoch 45:3; 48:2–3

"He shall be a staff to the righteous
by which they may lean and not fall.
He shall be the light of the nations,
and the hope of all who mourn in spirit.
All who dwell on earth
shall fall and worship before Him."
—1 Enoch 48:4–5

"And He sat on the throne of glory,
and the sum of judgment was given
to the Son of Man.
He will open all the hidden things;
for the Lord of Spirits has chosen Him.

He was concealed in the presence of YHWH
before the world was created
and will be revealed to the righteous
in the appointed time."
—1 Enoch 62:2, 7

"He preserved the remnant
for His mercy's sake.
And you, O Ezra,
lay up in your heart the signs
that I have shown you,
and the dreams that you have seen,
and the interpretations that you have heard.
For you shall be taken up from among men,
and remain with My Son
until the times are ended."
—4 Ezra 13:48–50

Final Seal

The Undefiled Will Not Be Defiled

The dust of the earth may rage.
The tongues of men may slander.
The powers of the age may conspire.

But the Undefiled One remains.

No lie can touch His Name.
No blasphemy can mar His glory.
No rebellion can dim His light.

He is the Flame untouched by time.
The Word unbroken by war.
The King of kings unmoved by thrones of men.

The slanders of the nations
will fall silent.
The accusations of the deceivers
will be burned away.
The mockery of the proud
will be swallowed by the roar
of the King's return.

The Undefiled will not be defiled.
The Holy One will not be profaned.
The Lamb who was slain now reigns,
crowned with incorruptible honor.

His Name endures.
His Throne endures.
His Kingdom endures.

This scroll closes
but the vindication of the Undefiled One
has only begun.

Another scroll is already stirring
written not by the will of men,
but by the fire of heaven.

A vindication for the Name they slandered.
A sword for every lie they dared to forge.
A trumpet that will shatter the silence
of this fading age.

Every insult will fall.
Every false word will be consumed.

The One they mocked will arise
in unveiled majesty

crowned with many crowns,
robed in unstoppable light.

His Name will thunder across the heavens.
His glory will cleanse the earth.

The next unveiling is nearer than they know.

Watch.
Wait.
Burn awake.

The witness is not finished.
The echo is already stirring
in the bones of the earth.
The silence they trusted
is already breaking.

The Name they tried to silence
is already stirring.

The Undefiled One is coming
and every knee shall bow,
every tongue shall confess:

Yeshua haMashiach is YHWH
now and forevermore!

Acknowledgment

To the One with many glorious Names,
the **I AM** before Abraham was,

the Root of David,
the Bright Morning Star,
the Lion of Judah,
the Lamb without blemish,
the King of Kings, the Lord of Lords,
the Wonderful Counselor,
the Mighty God,
the Everlasting Father,
the Prince of Peace.

My YHWH Esh Okhlah, the Consuming Fire,
YHWH Tsidqenu, Our Righteousness,
Elohei Kedoshim, God of Holiness,
YHWH Mekaddishkem, YHWH Who Sanctifies,

The One Who is Incorruptible. (Romans 1:23)

This scroll is Yours.
This witness is Yours.
This vindication is Yours.

You alone are worthy
of every breath,
every inked line,
every trembling heart.

May Your undefiled glory be seen,
Your undefiled Name be honored,
Your undefiled Kingdom come.

All glory and honor and majesty
to the Undefiled One,
the Ancient of Days,
now and forever,

YHWH Yeshua.

About the Author

Sahar Soltani is not a watchman by title,
nor a prophet by claim.
She is simply a vessel,
broken and redeemed,
chosen to see
what others ignored,
entrusted with wisdom
not born of herself,
sharpened with discernment
not taught by men,
and compelled to speak truth
by the Ruach haQodesh alone
in an age that trades it for comfort.

Born of dust
yet called to the fire,
she writes not for applause,
but for the Audience of One.

Her works are not polished
with the pride of academia,
but forged in the secret wrestlings
between soul and Spirit.

She does not claim to be righteous,
only redeemed.
She does not claim to be flawless,
only faithful to the Light she was given.

To the seekers of truth,
to the wounded,
to the remnant,
these writings are given.

Not as a monument to herself,
but as a testimony
and a return
to the only worthy
Undefiled One.

www.ingramcontent.com/pod-product-compliance
Lightning Source LLC
Chambersburg PA
CBHW020342010526
44119CB00048B/566